"How-to" Instructions & Project Ideas

Hawaiian Punch Art

Creating 3-D Art with Paper Punches

Designed & Created by Janice L. Nishimoto

Written and Edited by:
Fuji Schenck-Murakami, Cathy Pascual Veillard
Janice L. Nishimoto and Christopher J. Wong

Design, Layout & Photographs by Cathy P. Veillard
Cover Design by Maggie Kunkel of KunkelWorks

ISBN 0-9724488-0-2

Printed in Hawaii

Acknowledgements

"Mahalo" to the following individuals, who each made a contribution in their own special way, towards the success of this book and especially this art:

Stanley Nishimoto
Christopher J. Wong
Maggie Kunkel
Alana Federico

Suppliers

We would like to acknowledge the following companies, for developing such wonderful products, which allowed us to create the beautiful floral designs featured in this book:

CarlaCraft™ Punches
Pergamano®
Making Memories®

Dedication

To our sons & daughter…
Sheri Nishimoto
Christopher J. Wong
Steven Nishimoto
Nicholas Murakami

You are our inspirations...
Love,
- Your Moms -
Janice, Fuji and Cathy

All rights reserved. No part of this publication may be reproduced or transmitted in any form or by any means, electronic or mechanical, including photocopying, recording or by any information storage and retrieval system, without written permission of the copyright holder.

© 2002 by Album Artistry
Album Artistry
98-751 Naalii St.
Aiea, Hawaii 96701
Ph: (808) 484-9480

Website:
www.albumartistry.com

Table of Contents

Tools & Supplies 4

Craft Punches - Checklist 5

Plumeria 6

Anthurium 7

Hibiscus 8-9

Flower Leaves 9

Heliconia 10-11

GALLERY 12-13

Orchid 14-15

Ginger 16

Parrot's Beak 17

Bird of Paradise 18-19

Rose 20-21

Ume (Plum Blossom) 22

Sakura (Cherry Blossom) 23

Kikyou (Bell Flower) 24

Monstera:
Also known as "Windowleaf" or "Split-leaf Philodendron". Originating from Mexico & Guatemala, the plant is an avid "jungle tree climber" in the wild. Its large, glossy leaves are deeply splitted with oblong-shaped holes.

Monstera is popularly used in tropical gardens as a "backdrop" to enhance the colors of other flora. For this reason, we have selected the *Monstera* to provide a setting for this book as well; to highlight the exquisite detail and colors of each "punched" flower featured in the pages to follow.

Tools & Supplies

Craft Punches by CarlaCraft™

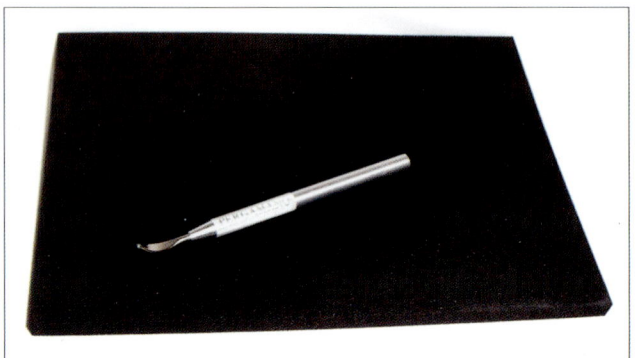

Embossing tool Hockey Stick (art.nr.1100)
and Perforating pad Excellent (art.nr.1419)
by Pergamano®

Twistel by
Making Memories®

Assorted mini plastic
and glass beads.

Assorted shapes of
Domed Window Cards

Assorted colors of velvet and vellum paper.

Basic Supplies: Cutting scissors, deckle scissors, colored chalks, gold 24 gauge wire, long tweezers, tacky glue, and fine felt-tipped markers *(not shown)*.

Craft Punches

The following is a list of CarlaCraft™ punches* used to create the flowers in this book. Use this list to keep track of your own punch collection. *(*Approximate sizes shown)*

☐ **SAKURA (L)**
Cherry Blossom

☐ **SAKURA (M)**
Cherry Blossom

☐ **UME (M)**
Plum Blossom

☐ **KIKYOU (M)**
Bell Flower

☐ **LEAF (M)**

☐ **SAKURA (XL)**
Cherry Blossom

☐ **UME (XL)**
Plum Blossom

☐ **KIKYOU (XL)**
Bell Flower

☐ **LEAF (XL)**

☐ **SAKURA (J)**
Cherry Blossom

☐ **UME (J)**
Plum Blossom

☐ **KIKYOU (J)**
Bell Flower

☐ **LEAF (J)**

☐ **HEART (L)**

☐ **HEART (M)**

☐ **SAKURA-A (XL)**
Cherry Blossom Petal

☐ **SAKURA-A (M)**
Cherry Blossom Petal

Hawaiian Punch Art

Plumeria

PUNCH:

- **Kikyou Flower:** Punch out one (1) flower from white vellum paper.

For a variation, use different Kikyou punch sizes.

Embellishments:
- Yellow chalk *(or desired color)*

Plumeria:
Also known as *Frangipani* or *Temple Tree*. The blossoms average 2-3 inches in diameter and come in white, red, yellow, pink or a multiple of colors. The very fragrant flowers are popular in Hawaii for lei-making.

Step 1: Between each petal, cut a "V" shaped slit halfway down towards the center.

Step 2: Trim and round off the tips of each petal.

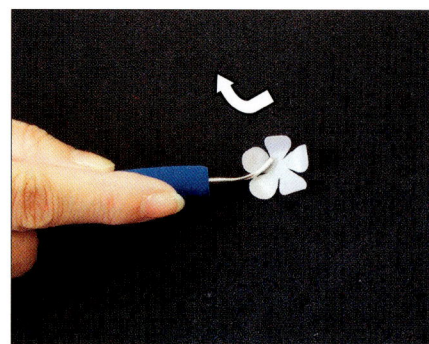

Step 3: Place flower on a foam pad and use the side of the hockey stick. Starting from the center of the flower - curl each petal by pressing towards you.

Step 4: Turn the flower over and apply pressure to the center with the tip of the hockey stick.

Step 5: With a cotton swab, lightly apply yellow chalk to the center of the flower, coloring to a desirable shade.

Anthurium

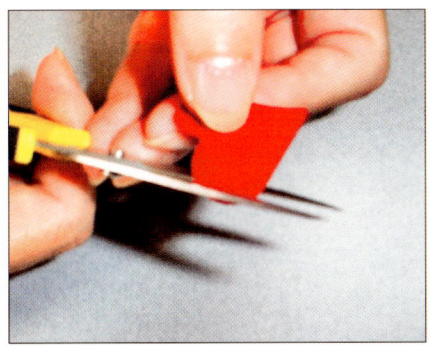

Step 1: Fold each heart and trim down on the edges. Discard excess.

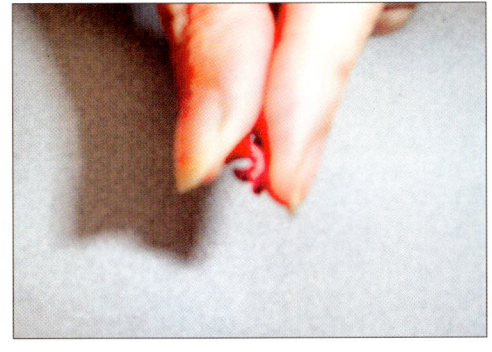

Step 2: Roll into a ball to crumple (this will give your flower its "texture").

PUNCH:

- **Heart (M):** Punch out one (1) heart from red velvet paper.
- For **Leaves (L)**, punch out from green velvet paper.

Embellishments:
- Yellow polymer clay
- Gold 24 gauge wire
- Green Twistel

Step 3: Take a small piece of polymer clay. Roll and shape to make the spadix, approx. 1/4" to 3/8" in length.

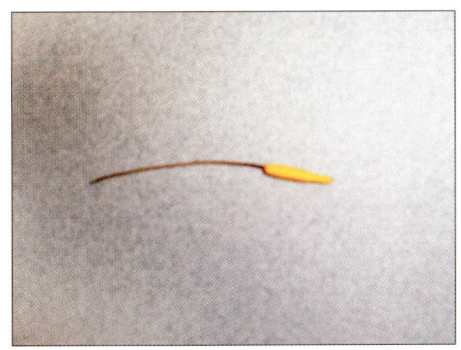

Step 4: Cut a 2" piece of wire and thread through one end of the spadix. Complete shaping if required. Bake as instructed on the clay package.

Anthurium:
Native to South America, the Anthurium was introduced to Hawaii in 1889. The shiny heart-shaped flower with its protruding spadix, lasts several weeks after cutting.

Step 5: Pierce a small hole in the middle of the flower.

Step 6: Thread the wire of the spadix through the flower.

Leaves: Follow steps 1 & 2

Hawaiian Punch Art 7

Hibiscus

PUNCH:

Ume Flower (XL):
Punch out one (1) flower from pink velvet paper.

Embellishments:
- Pink chalk (or any coordinating color)
- Six 5mm yellow beads
- Gold 24 gauge wire

Hibiscus:
Flowers are available in a variety of colors and have blossoms 2" to 12" in diameter. The yellow Hibiscus is Hawaii's state flower and the national flower of Malaysia. The Hibiscus does not last more than a day when cut, which is why it has earned its meaning as "delicate beauty".

Step 1: Cut a slit between each petal approximately 1/4" towards the center of the flower.

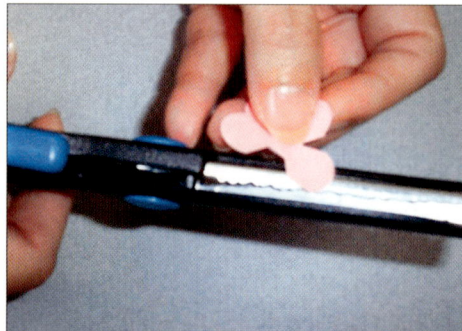

Step 2: Trim around each petal with a deckle scissor.

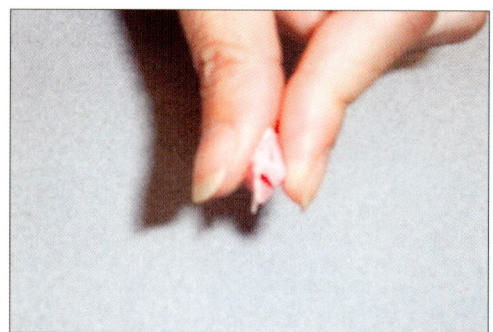

Step 3: Roll into a ball to crumple (this will give your flower petals its "texture".)

Step 4: Turn flower over and place on a foam pad. Use the side of the hockey stick and curl each petal by pressing from the center outwards.

Step 5: PISTOL: With gold wire, thread six yellow beads.

Step 6: Bend the wire in half making sure 3 beads are on each side of the fold. Twist the wire to hold the beads in place.

Hawaiian Punch Art

Close-up of flower and pistol.

Step 7: Using the pink chalk, lightly color the center of the flower to a desired shade.

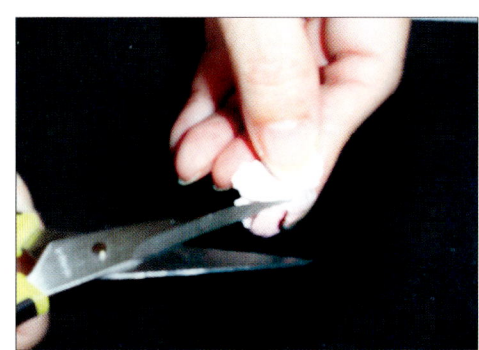

Step 8: Make a hole in the center of the flower and insert the pistol. Secure by gluing to background paper (i.e. greeting card, scrapbook).

Leaves

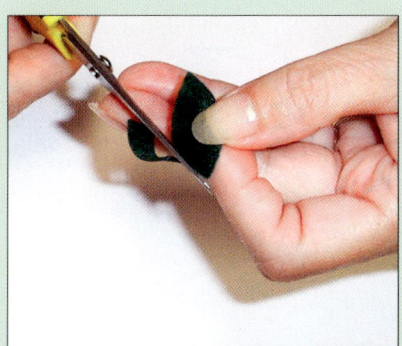

Step 1: Trim off one side of the petal, from the indentation to the tip. Discard excess.

Step 2: Cut several slits in an angle, on each side of the leaf.

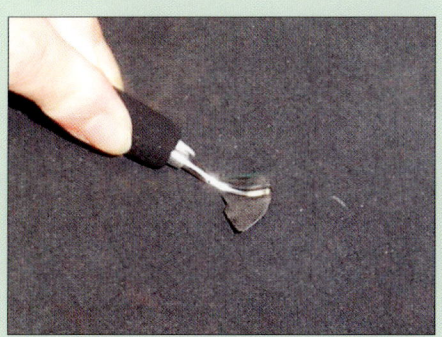

Step 3: Curl each leaf with the edge of the hockey stick on the foam pad.

Step 4: Twist to shape the leaf. Attach to your flower's stem (green or brown Twistel) and glue.

LEAVES for Bird of Paradise, Heliconia, Ginger and Parrot's Beak

PUNCH:

- **Sakura Petal (XL):** Punch out one (1) petal from green vellum or velvet paper in a shade which will compliment the color(s) of your flower.

Heliconia

PUNCHES:

- **Sakura Petal (XL):** Punch out 3-4 petals from red velvet paper.

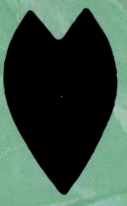

- **Sakura Petal (M):** Punch out two (2) petals from red velvet paper.

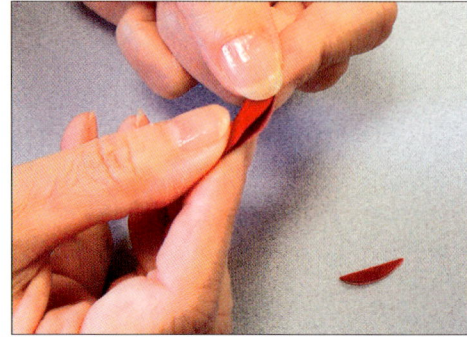

Step 1: Fold two **medium** petals, each in half, lengthwise.

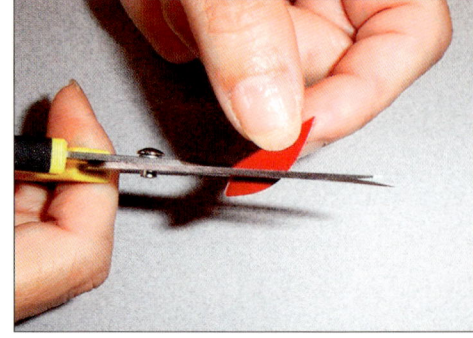

Step 2: Trim petals as illustrated, cutting one slightly smaller than the other.

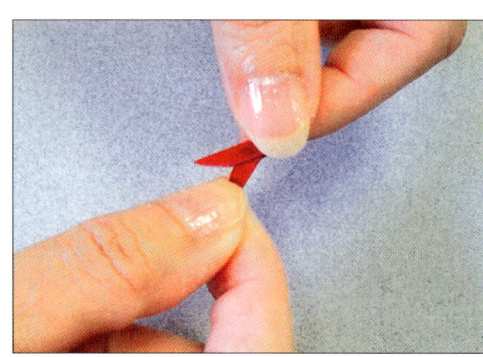

Step 3: Insert the larger end of one petal between the fold of the second petal to form a "V" and glue together. This will be the top of your flower.

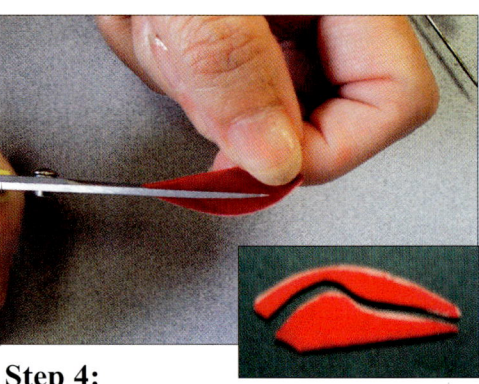

Step 4: Fold **large** petals in half lengthwise, and trim as shown in illustration. You will need 3-4 large petals according to your preference.

Step 5: Take the top petals, completed from **Step 3,** and insert between the fold at large end of one of the **large** petals from **Step 4** and glue.

Step 6: Trim the excess from the bottom.

10   Hawaiian Punch Art

Step 7: Glue another **large** petal to the opposite side of the previous petal.

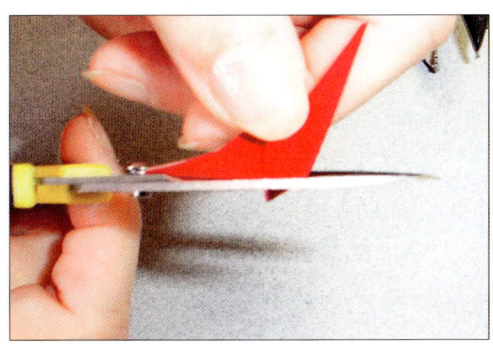

Step 8: Trim off any excess.

Step 9: Glue the last **large** petal on the adjacent side.

Note: You may add more petals if desired.

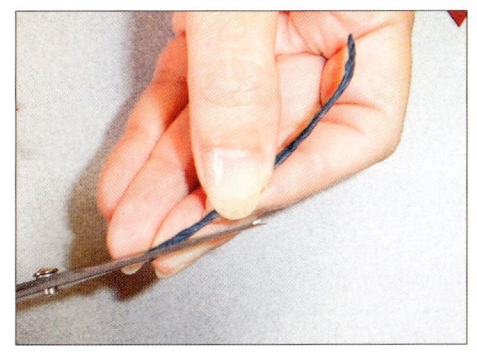

Step 10: For the stem, cut Twistel to desired length (approx. 3") and trim one end at an angle*.

*Note: Refer to "Parrot's Beak" - Step #3

Step 11: Glue the angled end of the Twistel to the back end of the last petal.

Step 12: Embellish with tiny white pearl beads and detail top edges of the petal with dark green chalk.

Embellishments:
- Tiny white pearl beads
- Dark green chalk
- Green Twistel
- **Leaves**: See page 9

Heliconia:
The Heliconia family's origin is South America. The Heliconia is named after Mt. Helicon, home of ancient Greek gods. They are related to the bananas, and range from three feet to over twenty feet tall. They are long lasting and used in Hawaiian tropical floral arrangements.

Hawaiian Punch Art

Gallery

12   Hawaiian Punch Art

Gallery

Hawaiian Punch Art   13

Orchid

PUNCH:

- **Sakura Flower (M or XL):** For each orchid, punch out two (2) flowers from dark orange vellum paper.

Embellishments:
- Red marking pen
- 5mm yellow beads

Orchid:
The orchid symbolizes love, beauty, wisdom and thoughtfulness. There are almost 25,000 varieties of orchids, more than any other type of flower.

Part I: Outside Petals

Step 1: Cut a slit between each petal approx. half way down on all sides.

Step 2: Trim down from the indentation of petal #3, creating a thinner petal.

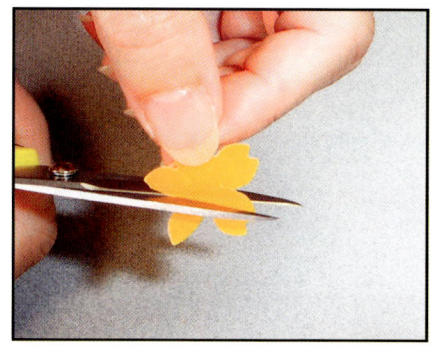

Step 3: Follow **Step 2**, trimming petal #3, on the opposite side.

Step 4: Repeat **Steps 2 & 3** to petals #4 and #1.

Step 5: Use deckle scissors to trim around petals #2 & #5.

Completed trimming of "outside" petal.

14 Hawaiian Punch Art

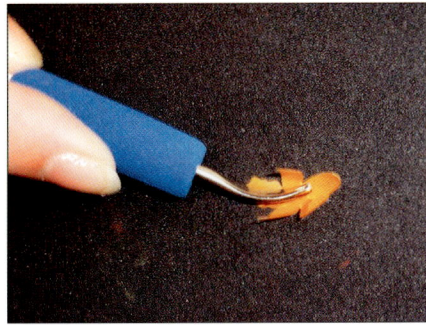

Step 6: Using the foam pad, curl each petal from the inside out using the side of the hockey stick.

Step 7: Flip flower over and press down on the center with the tip of the hockey stick.

Part II: Flower Center (Pistol)

Step 1: Cut two petals off the second Sakura.

Step 2: Use deckle scissors to trim around the two petals. Discard the other three petals.

Step 3: Curl the two petals using the side of the hockey stick.

Step 4: Using a tweezer, shape the two petals to form a cone and carefully glue to secure.

Step 5: Glue the cone-shaped petals to the center of the outside petals.

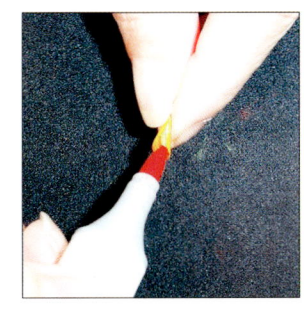

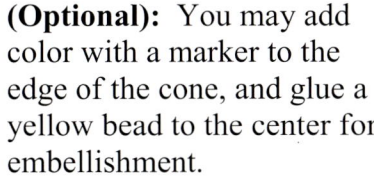

(Optional): You may add color with a marker to the edge of the cone, and glue a yellow bead to the center for embellishment.

Hawaiian Punch Art 15

Ginger

PUNCH:

- **Kikyou Flower (XL):** Punch out five (5) flowers from pink velvet paper.

Embellishments:
- Green Twistel
- White mini beads
- **Leaves:** See page 9

Ginger:
The Ginger family is native to the Western Pacific. The Ginger come in an array of colors, the most popular being red and pink. The root of the Ginger plant is used for spices and herbs.

Step 1: Divide by cutting a Kikyou flower punch into three segments. Make one 1-petal and two 2-petal segments, from each flower punch.

Step 2: Using the foam pad, curl all petals with the side of the hockey stick, velvet side down.

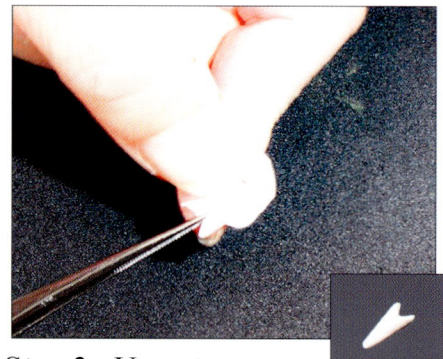

Step 3: Use a tweezer to make a cone with one of the 1-petal segments; wrap another 1-petal segment around it and glue. This will be the center of your flower.

Step 4: Fold the 2-petal segment in half and place the cone tips in the middle. Glue to secure.

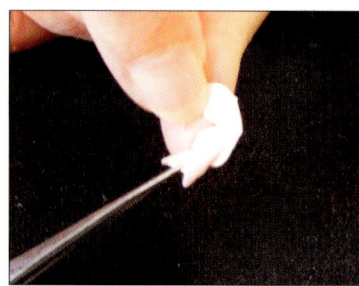

Step 5: Fold another 2-petal segment in half. Place the cone tips in-between and glue. Wrap the petals around the cone and glue the petals where they meet.

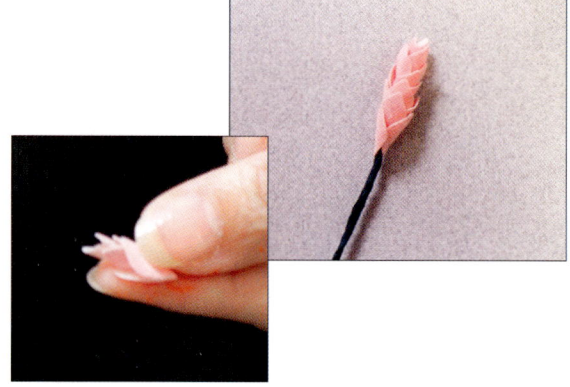

Step 6: Glue remaining 2-petal segments, as in **Step 5**, alternating the flower petals.

STEM: Insert and attach a green Twistel to the bottom of the flower before gluing the final layer.

Optional: *Embellish with a few mini white beads between the petals.*

Parrot's Beak

PUNCHES:

- **Sakura Petal (XL):** Punch one (1) petal from red velvet paper.

- **Sakura Petal (M):** Punch out two (2) petals from red velvet paper.

Embellishments:
- Orange Twistel
- Black Marking Pen
- Green Twistel
- **Leaves:** See page 9

Parrot's Beak:
This is the most commonly grown heliconia in Hawaii. It was introduced to Hawaii from Puerto Rico in 1950. The Heliconia Psittacorum, meaning of the parrot, describes the black and orange flower shaped like the beak of a parrot.

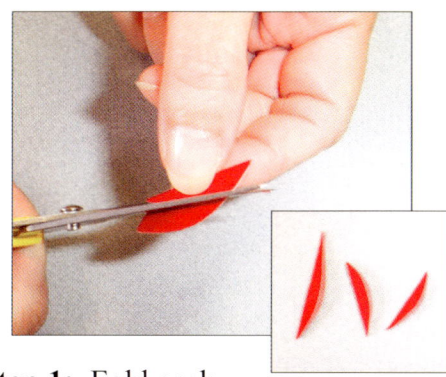

Step 1: Fold each petal in half and trim as shown.

Note: Refer to "Heliconia" - Step #2

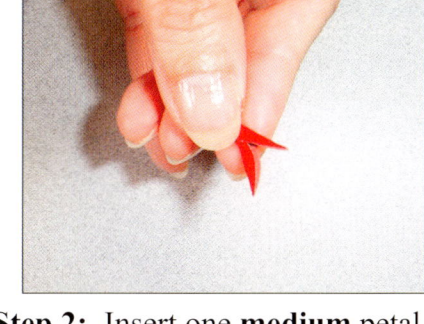

Step 2: Insert one **medium** petal, in the fold of the **large** petal, placing it 1/3 from the top. Position the second **medium** petal, approx. 1/3 below the first **medium** petal. Glue to secure all petals together.

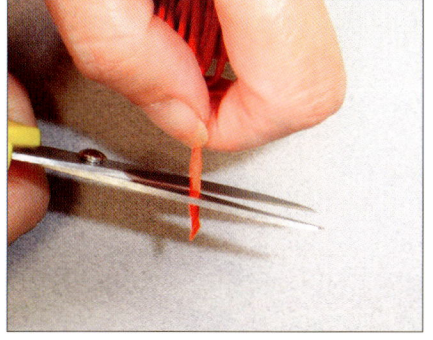

Step 3: Cut orange Twistel with one end of each piece, cut at an angle. You will need 4-6 pieces, varying in lengths from 1/4" to 1/2".
(See enlarged sample)

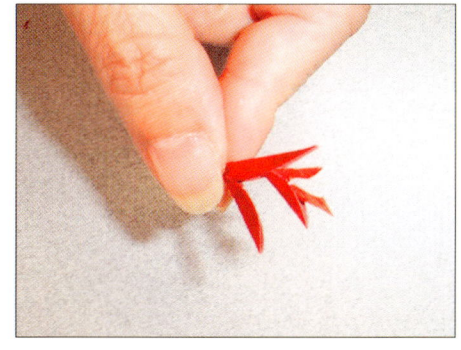

Step 4: Insert and glue, 2-3 pieces of Twistel as shown, in each of the **medium** petals.

Step 5: Color tips of each Twistel with a black marking pen.

Step 6: To complete, cut a 3" piece of green Twistel. Insert and glue at the base of your flower.

Hawaiian Punch Art 17

Bird of Paradise

PUNCHES:

- **Sakura Petal (XL):** Punch out one (1) petal from green velvet paper.

- **Sakura Petal (M):** Punch out three (3) petals from medium orange vellum, one (1) petal from bright orange vellum and two (2) from blue velvet paper.

Embellishments:
- Red Chalk
- Green Twistel
- **Leaves:** See page 9

Step 1: Fold green velvet paper petal in half. Trim into a curve as shown. The pointed end will be the front, and the raised portion, the rear. This will be called the "body".

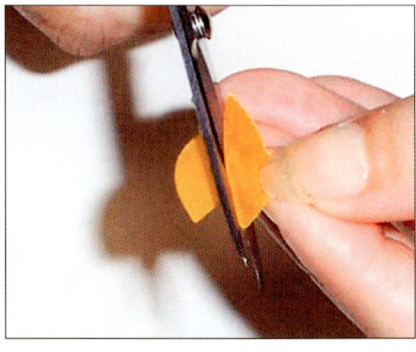

Step 2: From tip of petal, trim at a curve to a "V" shaped tip.

Step 3: Trim to make petals thin.

Tip: Use different shades of orange vellum. You should have seven (7) light orange petals and two (2) bright orange petals, for a total of nine (9) petals.

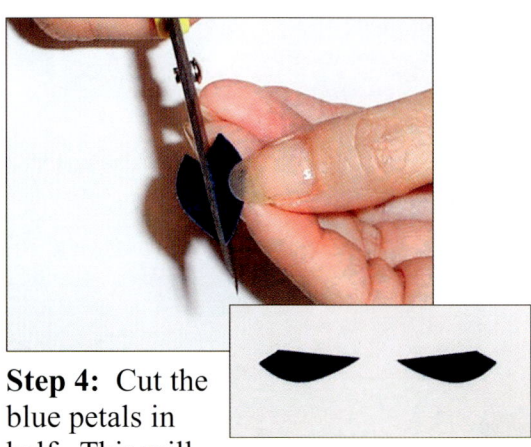

Step 4: Cut the blue petals in half. This will be called the "beak".

Step 5: Starting from the diagonal end, cut a small section off as shown.

18   Hawaiian Punch Art

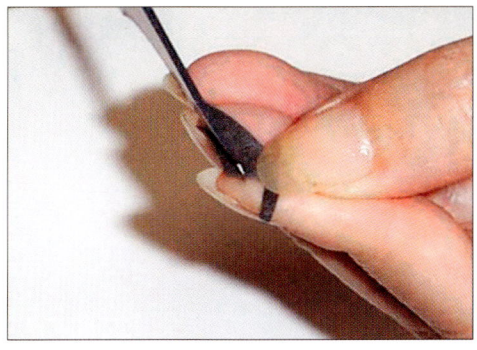 

Step 6: Trim along the straight-edge to form a thinner beak.

Completed body, petals and beaks.

Tip: You will need two (2) beaks facing the same direction to form one (1) flower.

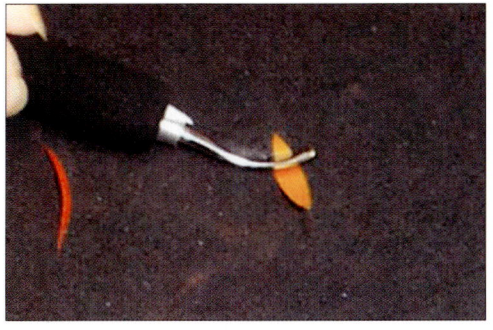 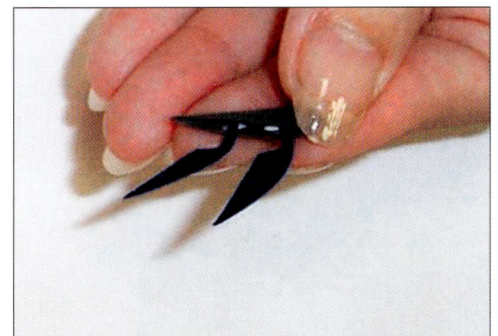

Step 7: Slightly curl all petals with a hockey stick.

Step 8: Insert two blue beaks into the green body; making sure the beaks face the front of the body.

Bird of Paradise: The Bird of Paradise is from Africa, but commonly used in Hawaiian tropical arrangements. The curved flower, with its orange and blue flower, resembles a long-necked bird.

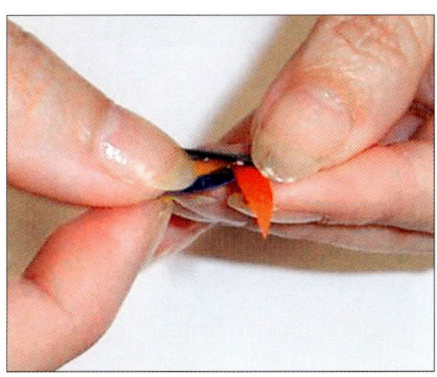 

Step 9: Apply glue to one end of each orange petal. Insert into the body with the curve of the petals facing backwards.

Embellish with red chalk around the edge of the body.

Bird of Paradise

Hawaiian Punch Art

Rose

PUNCH:

- **Ume Flower:**
  Punch three (3) flowers of the same size, from pink velvet paper.

Try a variation of the different sizes of the Ume shaped punches.

Embellishments:
- Pink chalk
- Pink marking pen

Rose:
The Rose is the national flower of the U.S.A. First bred in 1867 in France, the rose has been described as the "Queen of Flowers". Different meanings or languages have been given to some of the most popular colors of roses. *(See following page)*

Step 1: From one ume petal, cut two petals which will form a heart-shaped petal.

Step 2: From the second ume petal, cut a single petal into a "V" shape.

Step 3: Cut a slit, 3/4 of the way pass the center of the third ume.

Step 4: Place flowers, velvet side down, and curl outward with the hockey stick.

Step 5: Curl the heart-shaped petal into a cone with the tweezers; making sure the velvet side is on the outside.

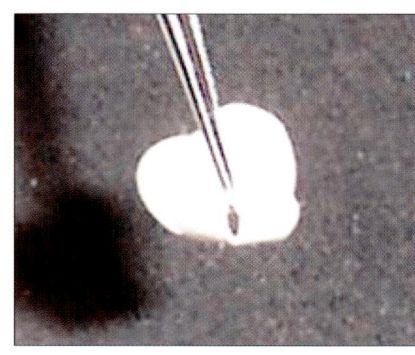

Step 6: Curl the 3-petal flower into a cone with the velvet side facing inward. Glue to adhere.

Step 7: Carefully apply glue to the tip of the first cone. Insert into the center of the second cone. With tweezers, curl the tips of the petals of the second cone outward.

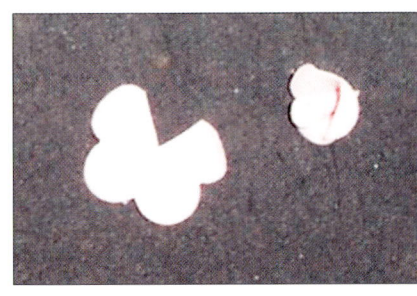

Step 8: Form another cone from the 4-petal flower.

Step 9: Apply glue to the tip of the second cone and insert into the newly formed cone. Offsetting the petals so it does not directly overlap. Curl tips of petals outward with tweezers.

Step 10: Create another cone from remaining flower. Apply glue to the tip of the third cone and insert into the last cone offsetting the petals so it does not directly overlap. Curl tips of petals outward with tweezers.

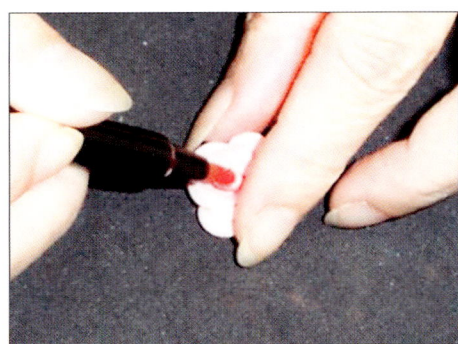

Step 11: Add desired color to center of rose with either markers or chalks.

Rose Color Meanings:

Red: Love, Respect

Light Pink: Admiration and Sympathy

Deep Pink: Gratitude and Appreciation

Yellow: Joy, Gladness

White: Innocence

Orange: Enthusiasm

Red and Yellow Blend: Joviality

Pale Blended Tones: Friendship

Lavender: Love at First Sight

Yellow and Red Edges: Falling in Love

Single Rose: Simplicity

Red Rosebuds: Purity

Rosebuds: Beauty, Youth

Red and White Roses in a Bunch: Unity for some people, bad luck for others.

Hawaiian Punch Art

Ume (Plum Blossom)

PUNCH:

- **Ume Flower (M):** Punch out one (1) flower from red velvet paper.

Embellishments:
- Tiny gold beads
- Brown Twistel

Ume:
One of Japan's most popular flower, the Ume is referred to the Japanese plum, Japanese flowering apricot. It was introduced from China in the 18th century. Ume trees can have red or pink blossoms as well as white, and have a delicate fragrance.

G. Murakami

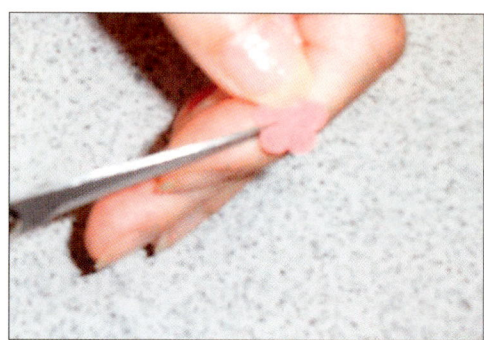

Step 1: Make a small cut between each petal halfway down towards the center of the flower.

Step 2: Place the flower on a foam pad and apply pressure on the center of the flower with the tip of the hockey stick.

Step 3: Apply craft glue to the center of the flower.

Step 4: Add tiny gold beads.

Make an Ume Flower Tree by arranging brown Twistels in the form of branches. Glue any number of Ume blossoms as desired.

Tip: You may also use a rubber stamp with a design of tree branches.

Sakura (Cherry Blossom)

Step 1: Cut a small slit between each petal.

Step 2: Place flower on a foam pad and curl each petal from the inside out, using the side of the hockey stick.

Step 3: Turn flower over and press down on the center of the flower with the tip of the hockey stick.

Step 4: Apply glue in the center of the flower and add tiny gold beads.

PUNCH:

- **Sakura Flower:** Punch out one (1) flower from pink vellum paper.

Try a variation of the different sizes of the Sakura shaped punches.

Embellishments:
- Tiny gold beads
- Brown Twistel

Sakura:
The Sakura, or Cherry Blossom, is Japan's national flower, and signifies the arrival of Spring. The Sakura opens all at once and seldom lasts more than a week.

Make a Cherry Blossom Tree by positioning brown Twistel in the form of branches. Glue various sizes of the flowers on branches according to your preference.

Tip: You can also use a rubber stamp with a branch design instead.

Hawaiian Punch Art

Kikyou (Bell Flower)

PUNCHES:

- **Kikyou Flower (XL):** Punch out one (1) petal from purple vellum paper.

Embellishments:
- Sm. white pearl bead
- Green Twistel

Kikyou:
The Kikyou is known as the Bellflower or Balloon flower which blooms from July to September. The name comes from the blue balloon buds which open into a five-pointed flower.

G. Murakami

Step 1: Cut a "V" shaped slit between each petal approx. half way down towards the center.

Step 2: Place flower on a foam pad and use the side of the hockey stick. Starting from the center of the flower, curl each petal towards you.

Step 3: Turn flower over and apply pressure at the center with the tip of the hockey stick.

Step 4: Embellish with a white pearl bead in the center of the flower.

Use green Twistel cut to different lengths for the stem.